# AVOIDING BURNOUT

*A Guide for Entrepreneurs, Artist, and Business Professionals to Gain & Maintain Success*

**Randy C. Reeves, II LMT**

Legal Notice

The purpose of this legal notice is to assert my rights and provide notice that the Book is protected by intellectual property laws, including copyright and trademark laws. I kindly request that you take note of the following points:

1. Copyright Protection: The Book, including its content, text, illustrations, images, and other creative elements, is protected by copyright under the laws of All countries. All rights are reserved to the author, Randy C. Reeves, II as the creator and owner of the Book.

2. Unauthorized Reproduction and Distribution: Any unauthorized reproduction, distribution, or dissemination of the Book, whether in physical or digital form, without the express written consent of the author, Randy C. Reeves, II, is strictly prohibited and may be subject to legal action.

3. Trademark Protection: The title "Avoiding Burnout: A Guide for Entrepreneurs, Artists, and Business Professionals to Gain and Maintain Success" is a trademark associated with the Book. Any unauthorized use of this trademark, including but not limited to the creation of derivative works or similar publications, is strictly prohibited.

4. Fair Use and Attribution: Any use of excerpts, quotes, or references from the Book must comply with the principles of fair use and must be properly attributed to the author, Randy C. Reeves, II and the Book, citing the source and title accurately.

5. Disclaimer: The Book is intended for informational purposes only and is not a substitute for professional advice. The author, Randy C. Reeves, II, and the publisher shall not be held liable for any damages or consequences arising from the use of the information contained in the Book.

6. Reservations: The author, Randy C. Reeves II, reserves all

rights not expressly granted in this legal notice.

We trust that you will respect the intellectual property rights associated with the Book. If you wish to seek permission for any use beyond the scope of fair use, or if you have any questions or concerns regarding the Book, its content, or its rights, please feel free to contact us at the provided contact information.

Your prompt attention to this matter is greatly appreciated. This legal notice does not waive any rights or remedies available to the author, Randy C. Reeves, II under applicable law, and we reserve the right to take appropriate legal action against any infringement or violation of the Book's rights.

Thank you for your understanding and cooperation.

Sincerely,

Randy C. Reeves, II

# Disclaimer

The information provided in the book "Avoiding Burnout: A Guide for Entrepreneurs, Artists, and Business Professionals to Gain and Maintain Success" is intended for general informational purposes only. The book is not a substitute for professional advice or personalized guidance, and readers are encouraged to consult with qualified professionals in their respective fields for specific and tailored advice.

The content of this book is based on the knowledge available up to the year 2023 and reflects the understanding of burnout, success, and self-care at that time. However, it is important to recognize that the fields of entrepreneurship, artistry, and business are constantly evolving, and new research, practices, and developments may have emerged since the book's publication.

The author and publisher have made diligent efforts to ensure the accuracy and reliability of the information presented in this book. However, they do not make any representations or warranties regarding the completeness, accuracy, suitability, or applicability of the content. The reader is responsible for evaluating the information in this book and determining its relevance to their own circumstances.

Any reliance on the information provided in this book is at the reader's own risk. The author and publisher shall not be held liable for any damages or consequences arising from the use of the information contained in this book.

Additionally, the stories, examples, and case studies included in this book are intended to illustrate certain principles and concepts.

Names, characters, places, and incidents may have been altered or fictionalized to protect the privacy of individuals or organizations.

Lastly, the mention of specific products, services, organizations, or individuals in this book does not imply endorsement or recommendation. The inclusion of such references is for illustrative purposes only and does not constitute an endorsement of their offerings.

Readers are encouraged to exercise critical judgment, seek professional advice when appropriate, and implement the information in this book in a manner that aligns with their unique situations and goals.

In summary, "Avoiding Burnout: A Guide for Entrepreneurs, Artists, and Business Professionals to Gain and Maintain Success" is a compilation of knowledge and insights as of 2023, and readers are advised to verify the currency of the information and adapt it to their current circumstances. The author and publisher disclaim any responsibility for the actions taken by readers based on the content of this book.

# Introduction

In the relentless pursuit of success, entrepreneurs, artists, and business professionals often find themselves entangled in a fast-paced and demanding world—a world that can lead to the perilous edge of burnout. As dreams are chased and ambitions ignited, the constant juggling of responsibilities and expectations can exact a toll on our physical, emotional, and mental well-being. Yet, within the crucible of our endeavors lies the key to sustainable success—the art of avoiding burnout and preserving our vitality.

Welcome to "Avoiding Burnout: A Guide for Entrepreneurs, Artists, and Business Professionals to Gain and Maintain Success." This book is not just a manual for survival—it is a compass that empowers individuals to navigate their professional journeys with wisdom, resilience, and self-care.

In the pages that follow, we embark on a transformative exploration of burnout—the silent adversary that threatens to erode the pillars of our success. Through poignant stories, expert insights, and practical strategies, we uncover the warning signs, causes, and impact of burnout. Armed with this knowledge, we journey into the realm of self-care, discovering its transformative power as an anchor for well-being and a catalyst for greatness.

Moreover, we delve into the art of setting realistic goals, empowering readers to achieve their aspirations while avoiding the traps of overexertion and overwhelm. From work-life integration to cultivating resilience in the face of challenges, we explore the essential components that foster a sustainable path to success.

As we embark on this empowering odyssey, let "Avoiding Burnout" serve as a guiding light—a testament to the inherent strength that lies within us all. Together, let us embrace a harmonious blend of ambition and self-care, leading to a life of fulfillment, prosperity, and unwavering success.

This is more than just a guide; it is an invitation to reclaim our vitality and thrive in our chosen paths. The journey to avoiding burnout and attaining enduring success begins now.

# TABLE OF CONTENT

# CHAPTER 1

# BREAKTIME

"Burnout is not just about being too busy or feeling overwhelmed…It's feeling like your work has no purpose and you don't have support."
— *Richie Norton*

The mentality of most hardworking professionals and entrepreneurs as it comes to breaks/breaktime is one of unimportance and it's the wrong one to have. Whether you put 40 plus hours a week for someone else or have the no days off lifestyle of the entrepreneur you're wrong. Using breaktime efficiently and constructively is a basic element to incorporate your work life to combat against that monster we're all trying to avoid, BURNOUT! I mean let's be honest here, the reason you work the 40+ hours and except for the no days off life is either because the money and perks are good, or you love what you do and can't see yourself doing anything else with your time for money. Proper use of breaktime is just as important if not more as it is as your working hours.

Taking regular breaks allows oneself to step away from your work periodically. Taking breaks helps to refresh your mind, prevent mental exhaustion, and restore your creativity. Periodic breaks refer to scheduled pauses or intervals of rest that are taken during a certain period of continuous activity or work. These breaks are important as they help prevent burnout, improve concentration, increase productivity, and promote overall well-being. Periodic breaks can take different forms depending on the nature of the activity and individual preferences but often include short periods of relaxation, stretching, physical activity, or simply stepping away from the task at hand. They can be as short as a few minutes or as long as several hours, depending on the needs of the individual. The frequency and duration of the breaks may vary depending on the task, but they should be planned and incorporated into a routine to ensure their effectiveness.

Use your break to reassess your to-do list and prioritize tasks for the remainder of the day. This will help you stay organized and focused when you get back to work. If it's a sedentary type of work you're involved with then take a walk for your break. Walking around the office/workspace or going outside for some fresh air. This can help clear your mind, improve blood circulation, and boost your energy levels. If a walk isn't possible the next best thing is stretching. Sitting for long periods can cause muscle tension and stiffness. Use your break to stretch and loosen up your muscles. Simple stretches like neck rolls, shoulder shrugs, and wrist exercises can make a big difference. Organizing your workspace/desk an organized environment can reduce stress and improve productivity. Lastly eating on a break lies in its ability to replenish energy, enhance productivity, prevent burnout, improve mood, maintain health, and promote job satisfaction. Eating on break can positively impact your mood. Hunger and low blood sugar levels can lead to irritability, fatigue, and a negative mindset. Proper nourishment through a meal or snack stabilizes blood sugar levels, promoting a more positive and optimistic mindset. It is crucial to prioritize regular breaks for proper nourishment and self-care.

Meditation during your break can be a great way to relax, rejuvenate, and center yourself. Incorporating meditation into your break is simple.

You can start by first setting a timer for how long you would like to meditate. Start with shorter durations, like 5 or 10 minutes, and gradually increase the time as you get more comfortable with the practice. Find a quiet and comfortable space, get into a comfortable posture, close your eyes and focus on your breathing, notice the sensation from inhaling and exhaling. Be present and non-judgmental as thoughts, emotions, or sensations arise, acknowledging their presence without judgment. If you find yourself getting carried away with thoughts, gently redirect your focus back to your breath. Understand that meditation is not about achieving a perfectly clear mind or suppressing thoughts. It is a practice of cultivating awareness, acceptance, and compassion for yourself. Be patient with yourself and approach the practice with an open and non-judgmental attitude. Conclude your meditation when your timer goes off, slowly transition out of your meditation by taking a few deep breaths and gently opening your eyes. Take a moment to notice how you feel before resuming your activities. Remember, even a short meditation break can have significant benefits for your well-being and productivity, so don't hesitate to incorporate this practice into your daily routine.

Now with all this new discovered knowledge on the importance of breaktime and how to spend it, the next step is to apply it. Take these techniques to discover a regiment that best works for you and your work/business. This is only the first step but an important one, some things may work better than others but they're all helpful. Remember burnout happens over a length of time not overnight and taking proper break while you work will aid in the fight against burnout.

"Just because you take breaks doesn't mean you're broken."

**— Curtis Tyrone Jones**

**Things to Consider When Prioritizing Breaktime in Your Work Life:**

1. **Identify your priorities:** Understand your goals and tasks for the day. This will help you determine when and how long you can take breaks without compromising your productivity or deadlines.

2. **Plan:** Create a schedule that includes designated break times. This will ensure that you have allocated time for relaxation and rejuvenation throughout the day.

3. **Break duration:** Determine the ideal length of breaks based on your needs and work demands. Short, frequent breaks (e.g., 5-10 minutes every hour) can help maintain focus, while longer breaks (e.g., 30 minutes to an hour) can provide a more significant opportunity to recharge.

4. **Intentional breaks:** Use your breaks wisely. Engage in activities that help you relax and recharge, such as going for a walk, meditating, stretching, or engaging in a hobby. Avoid activities that may drain your energy, such as excessive screen time or mindlessly scrolling through social media.

5. **Listen to your body:** Pay attention to your energy levels and focus throughout the day. Take breaks when you feel mentally fatigued or physically tired. Pushing through without breaks may lead to decreased productivity and burnout.

6. **Schedule breaks during low-energy periods:** Aim to take breaks during times when your energy naturally dips, such as mid-morning or mid-afternoon. This can help you optimize your productivity by allowing yourself to recharge during these typically less productive periods.

7. **Prioritize quality breaks over quantity:** Focus on the quality of your breaks rather than trying to take as many breaks as possible. Even a short, focused break with a specific purpose can be more beneficial than multiple unfocused breaks.

8. **Communicate with colleagues:** If you are part of a team or have colleagues who rely on your availability, communicate your break schedule to ensure a smooth workflow and avoid any misunderstandings.

9. **Set boundaries:** Establish clear boundaries between yourself and others regarding interruptions during your designated break times. Avoid checking emails or responding to work-related messages during breaks

to fully detach and recharge.

10. **Evaluate and adjust**: Regularly assess the effectiveness of your break schedule. Recognize which break durations and timing work best for you and adjust if needed to enhance your overall work-life balance and productivity.

# CHAPTER 2

# SETTING REALISTIC GOALS

*"The trouble with not having a goal is that you can spend your life running up and down the field and never score."*
**—Bill Copeland**

Setting goals for your work life is more fundamentally necessary than you think they are. Setting goals helps to provide focus and direction, increases motivation, and enables you to measure your success. Goal setting is the process of defining specific objectives and creating a plan to achieve them. It involves determining what you want to achieve, breaking it down into smaller, actionable steps, setting a timeline, and monitoring your progress. Where most people go wrong when it comes to setting goals is that the goals being set aren't realistic enough to achieve. By being realistic when setting goals, you increase your chances of success, maintain motivation, and ultimately achieve what you set out to accomplish.

Being realistic when setting goals is important for several reasons. One of the most essential reasons is the goal you set keeps you motivated and confident. Realistic goals promote sustainable progress. When you set achievable goals and start to experience gains in your endeavors, you build your confidence, self-esteem, and belief in your abilities. This positive reinforcement helps you stay motivated and fuels further progress. Realistic goals promote sustainable progress. Setting achievable milestones allows you to make steady progress and maintain momentum. Unrealistic goals may lead to burnout or inconsistency, as you may feel overwhelmed or disheartened by the lack of progress. This is when our time and resources must come into action. By having realistic goals set one can consider your available time, skills, and resources. These are considered the limitations and constraints that may exist in your life, such as work commitments, family responsibilities, or financial constraints. By being realistic, you can better plan and allocate your time and resources effectively, increasing your chances of achieving your goals. Remember at this point we are still training yourself in what it takes to avoid the BURNOUT!

Also, the fundamental aspect to avoid burnout through developing realistic goal setting regiment to your professional life is Adaptability. Setting realistic goals allows for flexibility and adaptability. Life is unpredictable, and obstacles and challenges may arise along the way. By setting realistic goals, you can adjust your plans and strategies as needed, making it easier to overcome obstacles and stay on track. Whatever it is that you are trying to achieve is purposeful and profitable to you and others. As you start to live by the realistic goals mindset and knowledge that nothing is built in a day but over time all the realistic goals you work for get achieved and always will. Staying positive when a realistic goal you set for your business or professional life fails can be challenging, but it's essential to maintain a positive mindset in order to bounce back and learn from the experience. Despite the setbacks you acknowledge your emotions it's 100% natural to feel disappointed, frustrated, or even discouraged when a goal fails.

The SMART (Specific, Measurable, Achievable, Relevant, Time-bound) framework is a powerful tool for setting realistic goals. This method ensures that each goal is well-defined and aligned with long-term objectives, while also providing a clear roadmap for achievement. Entrepreneurs, artists, and business professionals can apply the following principles of SMART goal setting to avoid burnout:

a. **Specificity:** Clearly define each goal with precise details, leaving no room for ambiguity. For instance, instead of setting a vague goal like "increase sales," be specific, such as "achieve a 15% increase in sales by the end of the quarter."

b. **Measurability**: Establish criteria for measuring progress and success. Measurable goals allow individuals to track their achievements, providing a sense of direction and motivation.

c. **Achievability**: Ensure that your goals are realistically attainable within your current resources and capabilities. Avoid setting goals that are too far-fetched, as they can lead to frustration and burnout.

d. **Relevance**: Align your goals with your overall vision and mission. Each goal should contribute directly to your larger purpose, ensuring that you are focusing on the most critical objectives.

e. **Time-bound**: Set clear deadlines for each goal, creating a sense of urgency and encouraging consistent effort.

Entrepreneurs, artists, and business professionals often have ambitious long-term goals. To prevent feeling overwhelmed, breaking down larger goals into smaller, manageable tasks is essential. This step-by-step approach allows individuals to focus on specific actions, one at a time, and celebrate incremental achievements along the way. While setting goals is crucial for professional growth, it is equally vital to prioritize self-care within the process. Entrepreneurs and professionals can incorporate self-care into their goal-setting practices by considering work-life balance, personal well-being, and mental health. Avoiding burnout requires acknowledging the importance of rest and rejuvenation alongside professional achievements.

Reflect and learn take the time to analyze what went wrong and identify the reasons for the failure. Soon after try to start focusing on all things positive down to just having breath in your lungs. DO NOT

DWELL BURNOUT IS AROUND THE CORNER! Set new goals and still being realistic even if you have a rush situation of some sort. Use the lessons learned from the failure to set new, revised goals. Incorporate the knowledge gained from the setback into your plans and develop a strategy to move forward. This gives you a fresh start and helps you regain your sense of purpose. Your next move is to seek support and surround yourself with positive, supportive individuals who can provide encouragement and motivation. Share your experiences and challenges with them, as they can offer different perspectives and help you regain confidence. Remember, failure doesn't define you or your capabilities. It's how you respond to failure that matters most. Maintaining a positive attitude and using the experience as a springboard for growth will help you navigate setbacks and continue the path to success.

"By recording your dreams and goals on paper, you set in motion the process of becoming the person you most want to be. Put your future in good hands—your own." —*Mark Victor Hansen*

**Things to Consider When setting realistic goals:**

1. **Self-Assessment:** Reflect on your strengths, weaknesses, and current capacity to determine what goals are achievable within your capabilities.

2. **Long-Term Vision:** Ensure that your goals align with your long-term vision and aspirations, creating a roadmap for your overall success.

3. **Specificity:** Clearly define each goal with specific details, leaving no room for ambiguity or misinterpretation.

4. **Measurability:** Set clear criteria for measuring progress and success, allowing you to track your achievements effectively.

5. **Achievability:** Ensure that your goals are realistically attainable given your available resources, skills, and time constraints.

6. **Relevance:** Align your goals with your values, mission, and the overall direction of your entrepreneurial venture, artistry, or

business.

7. **Time-Bound:** Set realistic deadlines for each goal, providing a sense of urgency and motivation to stay on track.

8. **Breaking Down Goals:** Divide larger goals into smaller, manageable tasks to avoid feeling overwhelmed and to celebrate incremental progress.

9. **Resource Evaluation:** Assess the resources, such as finances, manpower, and technology, required to achieve your goals realistically.

10. **Risk Assessment:** Identify potential obstacles and challenges that may arise and develop contingency plans to address them.

11. **Prioritization:** Rank your goals in order of importance and urgency, focusing on the most critical objectives first.

12. **Flexibility:** Remain open to adjusting your goals and strategies as circumstances change or new opportunities arise.

13. **Support System:** Seek support and feedback from mentors, peers, or professionals in your field to gain valuable insights and encouragement.

14. **Balancing Work and Life:** Ensure that your goals consider work-life balance, allowing time for personal well-being and rejuvenation.

15. **Celebrate Milestones:** Acknowledge and celebrate your achievements at various milestones, reinforcing your progress and boosting motivation.

16. **Avoiding Overcommitment:** Set realistic limits on the number of goals you pursue simultaneously to avoid spreading yourself too thin.

17. **Learning from Setbacks:** Embrace setbacks as learning opportunities and use them to refine your approach and grow as a professional.

18. **Self-Care Consideration:** Incorporate self-care practices into your goal-setting process, prioritizing mental and physical well-being.

19. **Accountability:** Hold yourself accountable for the progress toward your goals and seek assistance or feedback when needed.

20. **Stay Focused:** Avoid comparing your progress to others and stay focused on your unique journey and objectives.

# CHAPTER 3

# SELF-CARE

*"As you grow older, you will discover that you have two hands, one for helping yourself, the other for helping others."*

**-- Maya Angelou**

Is self-care a luxury or is it a priority? It is not a luxury; it is a priority when your goal is to avoid BURNOUT! While it is sometimes seen as indulgent or optional, self-care is essential for overall well-being and optimal functioning. Prioritizing self-care is crucial for maintaining physical, mental, and emotional health, and it plays a vital role in sustaining long-term success and fulfillment in all aspects of life, including as an entrepreneur.

Before discussing the priority of self-care, it is essential to address common myths that perpetuate the idea of self-care as a luxury:

a. **Time:** One myth is that self-care requires vast amounts of time, which many believe they cannot spare in their busy lives. Self-care can be practiced in small, regular doses and tailored to individual schedules.

b. **Cost:** Another misconception is that self-care requires spending a significant amount of money on extravagant activities. Self-care can be simple, inexpensive, and accessible to everyone.

c. **Selfishness:** Some individuals believe that prioritizing self-care is selfish, neglecting the needs of others. However, self-care is not about neglecting responsibilities but rather refueling oneself to better care for others.

Self-care encompasses a wide range of practices and activities that nurture and rejuvenate the mind, body, and spirit. It includes actions such as getting enough sleep, exercising, eating nourishing meals, taking breaks, engaging in hobbies, practicing mindfulness, seeking social support, and setting boundaries. These practices are not frivolous or self-indulgent; they are necessary for maintaining a healthy work-life balance, reducing stress, preventing burnout, and enhancing overall quality of life.

When you prioritize self-care, you are investing in your well-being and capacity to perform at your best. By taking care of yourself, you can increase your productivity, creativity, and effectiveness in your entrepreneurial pursuits. Self-care also helps to prevent the negative consequences of neglecting personal needs, such as increased stress, diminished mental and physical health, strained relationships, and impaired decision-making.

It's important to recognize that self-care is not selfish. Taking care of yourself allows you to show up fully for others and fulfill your responsibilities with greater energy and presence. It enables you to maintain a healthy work-life balance, prioritize your values, and nurture your relationships.

Not prioritizing self-care as a hardworking professional or entrepreneur can have several negative consequences. It can result in increased stress and BURNOUT. Ignoring self-care can have detrimental effects on your mental and physical health. Lack of sleep, poor nutrition, and insufficient exercise can lead to increased risk of illness, reduced energy levels, and diminished cognitive function.   Neglecting self-care often means neglecting important relationships in your life. Constantly working and not taking time for personal connections can strain relationships with family, friends, and loved ones. This can lead to feelings of isolation and can negatively impact both your personal and professional life. You will almost certainly decrease productivity, impaired decision-making, limited creativity, and increased risk of mental health issues. It is crucial to recognize the importance of self-care and take proactive steps to maintain a healthy balance between work and personal well-being for long-term success and fulfillment in your work.

In summary, self-care is not a luxury but a fundamental priority for overall well-being and success. It is essential for maintaining physical and mental health, preventing burnout, and optimizing your capacity to thrive in your professional life. By making self-care a priority, you invest in yourself and create a foundation for sustainable growth and well-being in both your personal and professional life.

*"It's not selfish to love yourself, take care of yourself, "and to make your happiness a priority. It's necessary." -**Mandy Hale***

**Self-care options that you should consider:**

1. Engage in regular exercise or physical activity that you enjoy, such as jogging, yoga, dancing, or playing a sport.

2. Practice mindfulness meditation or deep breathing exercises to promote relaxation and reduce stress.

3. Set aside time for hobbies or activities that bring you joy, such as painting, playing an instrument, gardening, or cooking.

4. Take breaks throughout the day to rest and recharge. Use these breaks to stretch, take a walk, or engage in a different activity to clear your mind.

5. Get enough sleep and establish a consistent sleep routine to ensure proper rest and rejuvenation.

6. Massage, Reflexology, Chiropractic adjustments for wellness, and other forms of bodywork.

7. Prioritize healthy eating by nourishing your body with balanced meals and incorporating fruits, vegetables, and whole grains into your diet.

8. Practice self-reflection and journaling to process your thoughts and emotions.

9. Connect with loved ones and spend quality time with family and friends. Plan activities or outings that promote social connection and support.

10. Schedule "me time" for self-care activities without distractions, such as reading a book, taking a bath, or pampering yourself.

11. Seek professional help or therapy if needed. Talking to a therapist can provide valuable support and guidance for your mental well-being.

12. Disconnect from technology and have dedicated periods of time without screens to reduce digital overload.

13. Practice gratitude by keeping a gratitude journal or expressing gratitude for the positive aspects of your life.

14. Listen to calming music or create a playlist that uplifts your mood and promotes relaxation.

15. Engage in acts of self-compassion and self-kindness. Treat yourself with understanding and care during challenging times.

# CHAPTER 4

# TIME MANAGEMENT

"Time isn't the main thing. It is the only thing."
*-Miles Davis*

Time management is a critical skill that plays a crucial role in not only our personal lives but also in our professional endeavors. In a fast-paced world where numerous responsibilities demand our attention, effective time management becomes paramount. It helps us prioritize tasks as well as better devote our efforts in avoiding BURNOUT!

One of the key aspects of time management is prioritizing tasks. By assessing the importance and urgency of each task, individuals can allocate their time and energy accordingly. This allows for a more balanced workload, preventing the accumulation of stress and exhaustion associated with burnout. Prioritization ensures that essential tasks are completed first and lesser-important ones can be addressed when there is more availability.

In addition to prioritization, time management allows individuals to set realistic goals and deadlines. Often when individuals take on too much, setting unrealistic expectations for themselves. By setting achievable goals and establishing reasonable timelines, individuals can work towards their objectives without feeling overwhelmed. This approach ensures that tasks are completed efficiently and without undue pressure, reducing an individual's chances of BURNOUT.

Another crucial aspect of time management is effective delegation. Many individuals hesitate to delegate tasks, fearing a loss of control or a decline in the quality of work. However, delegating tasks to others not only helps distribute the workload but also allows individuals to focus on more critical responsibilities. By avoiding the temptation to take on everything, individuals can ensure they do not stretch themselves too thin, thus minimizing the risk of burnout.

Furthermore, time management encourages individuals to schedule regular breaks and self-care activities. While it may seem counterintuitive, taking breaks enhances productivity by promoting mental and physical well-being. By incorporating time for relaxation, exercise, and hobbies into their schedule, individuals can replenish their energy reserves and reduce stress levels. This proactive approach to self-care is essential in preventing burnout.

Ultimately, effective time management is vital in avoiding burnout because it helps individuals maintain a healthy work-life balance. By organizing tasks, setting realistic goals, delegating when necessary, and incorporating self-care into their schedule, individuals can ensure that their time and energy are utilized efficiently. A well-managed routine allows individuals to work productively, avoid excessive stress, and prevent burnout from taking hold.

Burnout, a state of emotional, mental, and physical exhaustion caused by excessive and prolonged stress, has become increasingly common today. The demands of work, personal life, and other commitments can overwhelm even the most organized individuals. However, with proper time management, individuals can create a more manageable schedule and reduce the risk of burnout.

In conclusion, time management plays a crucial role in avoiding burnout. By prioritizing tasks, setting realistic goals, delegating responsibilities, and scheduling breaks, individuals can maintain a healthy work-life balance. Effective time management allows individuals to manage their workload efficiently, reducing stress and preventing exhaustion. Therefore, mastering time management skills is not only important for productivity and success but also for one's overall well-being and the prevention of burnout.

"Time = life; therefore, waste your time and waste of your life, or master your time and master your life." - *Alan Lakein*

**Things to Consider When it Comes to Prioritizing Time-Management:**

1. **Set clear goals:** Clearly define your short-term and long-term goals, both personal and professional. This helps you align your time and tasks with your overarching objectives.

2. **Prioritize tasks:** Determine the most important and urgent tasks that require your attention. Focus on high-priority activities that align with your goals and have the most significant impact on your business or creative work.

3. **Create a schedule or routine:** Establish a structured schedule or routine that includes designated time blocks for specific activities. This helps you allocate time for important tasks, including client meetings, creative work, administrative tasks, and personal activities.

4. **Identify time-wasting activities:** Identify activities that consume excessive time without adding much value to your business or creative endeavors. Minimize or eliminate these time-wasting activities to make room for more productive tasks.

5. **Delegate and outsource:** Identify tasks that can be delegated to others or outsourced to external professionals. Focus on your core strengths and responsibilities, and delegate non-essential or time-consuming tasks to free up your time for higher-value

activities.

6.  **Utilize productivity tools:** Explore and utilize productivity tools and apps that can help you manage your time effectively. These can include task management apps, calendar tools, project management software, and time tracking applications.

7.  **Practice effective communication:** Improve your communication skills to streamline interactions and minimize time spent on unnecessary discussions or misunderstandings. Be clear and concise in your communications to avoid miscommunication or lengthy back-and-forth exchanges.

8.  **Take regular breaks:** Allow yourself regular breaks throughout the day to rest and recharge. Short breaks can enhance focus and productivity, while longer breaks or vacations can prevent burnout and provide fresh perspectives.

9.  **Avoid multitasking:** While it may seem efficient, multitasking can lead to decreased productivity and increased errors. Focus on one task at a time, complete it, and then move on to the next. This helps maintain concentration and improves the quality of your work.

10. **Practice self-discipline and time boundaries:** Set boundaries for yourself and others regarding your time. Learn to say no to non-essential tasks or requests that may derail your schedule. Protect your time and prioritize what truly matters.

11. **Regularly review and reassess:** Regularly review your progress, evaluate your time management strategies, and make necessary adjustments. Reflect on what works well and what needs improvement to refine your approach.

12. **Foster a healthy work-life balance:** Prioritize time for personal activities, self-care, and quality time with loved ones. Balancing work and personal life promote overall well-being, happiness, and sustained success.

# CHAPTER 5

# SETTING BOUNDARIES

"Those who get angry when you set a boundary are the ones you need
to set boundaries for."

*– J.S. Wolfe*

Setting boundaries refers to the act of establishing limits or guidelines that define acceptable behaviors, actions, and expectations in various aspects of life, including personal relationships, professional settings, and one's own self-care practices. It involves communicating and enforcing these boundaries to ensure that individuals are respected, protected, and able to maintain their well-being, values, and priorities.

Contrary to popular belief, continuously working long hours does not necessarily equate to increased productivity. In fact, failing to set boundaries often leads to a lack of focus, decreased motivation, and reduced creativity. By establishing clear boundaries, professionals can create structured work schedules, allowing for adequate rest and recovery. Research has consistently shown that well-rested individuals are more productive, show heightened decision-making abilities, and yield better results in their respective fields.

Boundaries can be physical, emotional, or psychological in nature. They can encompass a wide range of areas, such as personal space, time management, workload, communication preferences, and respect for personal values and beliefs. Setting boundaries involves clearly communicating one's needs, limitations, and preferences to others, as well as defining the actions or behaviors that are considered acceptable or unacceptable.

One of the most apparent repercussions of not setting boundaries in your professional life is the erosion of a healthy work-life balance. Without clear boundaries, individuals may find themselves continuously tethered to their work, unable to disconnect and enjoy personal time. Consequently, this imbalance can lead to chronic stress, burnout, and a decline in overall well-being. Long working hours, late-night emails, and unchecked accessibility can disrupt personal relationships, neglect self-care, and leave individuals feeling overwhelmed and exhausted.

The purpose of setting boundaries is to establish healthy parameters that promote self-care, maintain personal integrity, and foster positive relationships. Boundaries help individuals maintain a sense of control, reduce stress, prevent burnout, and cultivate healthier interactions with others. They create a framework that allows individuals to prioritize their well-being, values, and goals, and to navigate various aspects of life with greater clarity and balance.

It is important to note that setting boundaries is a personal process and can vary from person to person. Boundaries should be respected and honored by both individuals and those with whom they interact. Regular evaluation and communication of boundaries are essential for maintaining their effectiveness and ensuring that they align with personal growth and changing circumstances.

Failing to establish and maintain boundaries in your professional life can have profound consequences on various aspects of your well-being. Whether it's a compromised work-life balance, reduced productivity and job satisfaction, strained relationships, or health issues, not setting clear limits can significantly impact both personal and professional realms. Recognizing the importance of setting boundaries is therefore essential for achieving a sustainable and fulfilling professional life, one that prioritizes physical and mental health, fosters strong relationships, and ensures overall happiness and success.

Remember, setting boundaries is an ongoing process that requires self-awareness, communication, and consistency. By considering these factors, you can establish boundaries that protect your well-being, promote work-life balance, and enable you to thrive both professionally and personally.

"Creating an atmosphere of mutual respect and consideration for boundaries, can lead you to the path of personal happiness." *-Nancy B. Urbach*

**Things to Consider When Setting Boundaries:**

1. **Define your values:** Understand your core values and what is important to you in your professional life. Use these values as a guide for establishing boundaries that align with your principles and priorities.

2. **Identify your limits:** Reflect on your personal limitations and capacity. Determine how much time, energy, and resources you can realistically devote to work-related tasks without compromising your well-being or other important areas of your life.

3. **Communicate clearly:** Articulate your boundaries in a clear and assertive manner. Communicate your expectations, availability, and limitations to colleagues, clients, and superiors to ensure that they understand and respect your boundaries.

4. **Set realistic goals and deadlines:** Establish realistic goals and deadlines that consider your workload and available resources. Avoid overcommitting and taking on more responsibilities than you can handle within a given timeframe.

5. **Establish working hours:** Define your working hours and communicate them to others. Make it clear when you are available and when you are not. Stick to these hours and avoid engaging in work-related activities outside of them unless necessary.

6. **Limit interruptions:** Minimize distractions and interruptions during focused work time. Use techniques like turning off notifications, closing unnecessary tabs, or utilizing tools to block distractions to maintain your focus and productivity.

7. **Delegate and say no:** Learn to delegate tasks to others and say no to requests or projects that do not align with your priorities or stretch you beyond your capacity. Be selective in the commitments you make to avoid overextending yourself.

8. **Schedule breaks and downtime**: Incorporate regular breaks into your schedule to recharge and prevent burnout. Set aside time for personal activities, hobbies, and self-care to ensure a healthy work-life balance.

9. **Protect personal time**: Establish boundaries around your personal time and avoid allowing work to encroach upon it. Prioritize your relationships, hobbies, and activities outside of work to maintain a sense of fulfillment and well-roundedness.

10. **Practice self-care**: Prioritize self-care activities such as exercise, relaxation, and time for personal well-being. Make self-care a non-negotiable part of your routine and set boundaries around it to ensure that it remains a priority.

11. **Seek support and accountability**: Surround yourself with individuals who respect your boundaries and support your efforts. Find an accountability partner or mentor who can help you stay on track and encourage you to maintain your boundaries.

12. **Regularly reassess and adjust**: Review your boundaries periodically and adjust as needed. As circumstances change, it is important to reassess and ensure that your boundaries remain

effective and aligned with your evolving needs and goals.

# CHAPTER 6

# INSPIRATION

"It takes wisdom to gain wealth without losing health."

*— Mokokoma Mokhonoana*

Inspiration acts as fuel for our minds and souls, driving us to push boundaries, chase our dreams, and achieve greatness. It bestows upon us the power to overcome challenges, turning ordinary individuals into extraordinary beings. However, true inspiration is not a fleeting moment, but rather a constant state of being. In this chapter we will explore the significance of finding ways to get inspired and, more importantly, to stay inspired.

Harnessing the Power of Inspiration is the catalyst that propels us forward, breathing life into our ideas and aspirations. It ignites a fire within us, awakening dormant potential. The power of inspiration lies in its ability to light the path towards our goals, enabling us to overcome obstacles with unwavering determination.

Despite its eminent potential, inspiration often remains elusive. Therefore, we must proactively seek ways to invite inspiration into our lives, ranging from creating conducive environments to cultivating a positive mindset. Surrounding ourselves with diverse sources of inspiration, such as literature, music, art, and nature, enhances our ability to spark ideas and fuel our passions.

Staying inspired is a powerful and transformative practice that fuels motivation, perseverance, and a sense of purpose. This chapter delves into the significance of maintaining inspiration in our lives, exploring its impact on various aspects of our existence and how it empowers us to overcome challenges, embrace change, and strive for greatness.

One might argue that finding short bursts of inspiration is sufficient to get through certain tasks or projects. However, staying inspired offers numerous long-term benefits that propel us towards success and personal fulfillment. It helps us maintain focus, persevere through challenges, and ensure consistent progress towards our goals.

Staying inspired involves fostering a mindset that allows us to continually seek and attract inspiration. By cultivating an attitude of gratitude, we develop an ability to recognize and appreciate the beauty and wonder in everyday life. Through mindfulness and self-reflection, we can analyze our goals and aspirations, connecting deeply with what truly motivates us. This introspection acts as an anchor, guiding our decisions and keeping us inspired even during difficult times.

The Power of Inspiration in Different Fields is an invaluable resource for individuals across various domains. In the arts, creative individuals draw inspiration from their surroundings, experiences, and emotions, translating them into tangible and intangible works that captivate audiences and provoke profound emotions. In science and technology, inspiration lies at the heart of groundbreaking innovations, as inventors and scientists are driven by their curiosity and their desire to push the boundaries of knowledge. Furthermore, in entrepreneurship and leadership, inspiration empowers individuals to build influential companies, lead teams, and impact communities positively.

In a world full of distractions and obstacles, finding ways to get inspired and, more importantly, staying inspired is paramount to realizing our fullest potential. Inspiration has the power to transform ordinary lives into extraordinary journeys. By immersing ourselves in diverse sources of inspiration and cultivating a mindset that keeps our inner flame burning, we can harness this power to create positive change in our lives and inspire others around us. Remember, inspiration is not simply a luxury but a necessity, enabling us to shape our world and leave a lasting impact. So, seek inspiration, let it fuel your dreams, and let it empower you to achieve greatness.

"You can't use up creativity. The more you use, the more you have."
*– Maya Angelou*

**Things to Consider:**

1. **Take a Break:** Step away from your usual routine and allow yourself some time to rest and recharge. Engage in activities that you enjoy, whether it's spending time in nature, reading a book, or pursuing a hobby.

2. **Seek Support:** Talk to friends, family, or colleagues who understand and empathize with your situation. Sharing your feelings can provide emotional support and a fresh perspective.

3. **Reflect on Past Successes:** Remind yourself of the achievements and triumphs you've experienced in the past. Reflecting on your successes can boost your confidence and motivation.

4. **Practice Mindfulness:** Engage in mindfulness practices like meditation or deep breathing exercises to reduce stress and bring awareness to the present moment.

5. **Seek Inspirational Content:** Watch motivational videos, read books or articles that inspire you, or listen to podcasts that share stories of resilience and success.

6. **Connect with Inspirational Figures:** Seek out inspiring individuals in your field or other areas of interest. Learn from their experiences and absorb their passion and dedication.

7. **Attend Workshops or Seminars:** Participate in workshops or seminars related to your profession or interests. Engaging with like-minded individuals and learning from experts can reignite your passion.

8. **Explore New Avenues:** Consider exploring new interests or activities outside of your regular work. Trying something different can stimulate creativity and inspire new ideas.

9. **Set Short-term Goals:** Instead of focusing on long-term objectives, set smaller, achievable goals that can provide a sense of accomplishment and progress.

10. **Surround Yourself with Positivity:** Spend time with positive and supportive individuals who uplift your spirits and encourage you to overcome challenges.

11. **Keep a Journal:** Write down your thoughts and feelings regularly to process your emotions and gain clarity about your situation. This can help you identify patterns and triggers for burnout.

12. **Practice Self-Compassion:** Be kind to yourself and acknowledge that burnout is a common experience. Treat yourself with the same compassion you would extend to a friend facing similar challenges.

13. **Seek Professional Help:** If burnout is severe or persistent, consider seeking help from a mental health professional who can provide guidance and support.

Remember, finding inspiration is a personal journey, and different methods may resonate with different individuals. Experiment with various strategies to see what works best for you in rekindling your motivation and overcoming burnout. Prioritizing self-care and well-being are essential during this process to ensure sustainable and fulfilling success in your personal and professional life.

# CHAPTER 7

# SELF-REFLECTION

"He that knows himself, knows others."
*– Charles Caleb Colton*

What is self-reflection actually? Well, it's the process of examining and evaluating one's own thoughts, emotions, and behaviors. It involves introspection and conscious thinking about one's own actions and experiences, as well as the underlying beliefs and values that shape them. Self-reflection promotes self-awareness and personal growth by allowing individuals to gain insight into their strengths, weaknesses, motivations, and aspirations. It often involves asking oneself questions and engaging in thoughtful and honest analysis to gain a deeper understanding of oneself and make positive changes.

In the journey of life, inspiration serves as a guiding light, illuminating the path towards personal growth, creativity, and fulfillment. Staying inspired is a powerful and transformative practice that fuels motivation, perseverance, and a sense of purpose. This chapter delves into the significance of maintaining inspiration in our lives, exploring its impact on various aspects of our existence and how it empowers us to overcome challenges, embrace change, and strive for greatness.

At the heart of inspiration lies the spark of creativity. When we stay inspired, our minds are open to new ideas, fresh perspectives, and innovative solutions. Inspiration fosters a dynamic flow of thoughts and encourages us to think beyond conventional boundaries. By staying connected to our creative core, we can innovate, problem-solve, and leave a lasting impact on the world around us.

Cultivating Motivation and resilience in the face of challenges and setbacks, inspiration acts as a reservoir of motivation and resilience. Inspired individuals find the strength to persevere and maintain unwavering determination. Inspirational stories of triumph over adversity remind us that obstacles are steppingstones to growth and that our dreams are worth pursuing, no matter the hurdles we encounter. Recognizing one's strengths can boost confidence and provide a foundation to excel in specific areas. Simultaneously, acknowledging areas for growth allows for targeted skill development and self-improvement.

When Learning from Mistakes and Failures Self-reflection encourages professionals to learn from their mistakes and failures, turning setbacks into valuable lessons. By analyzing what went wrong and why, individuals can implement corrective measures, adapt their strategies, and increase their resilience in the face of challenges. Regular self-reflection hones critical thinking skills, leading to more informed and thoughtful decision-making. By understanding their thought processes and biases, professionals can make better choices, weighing the potential consequences of their actions more effectively.

Self-reflection fosters emotional intelligence, enabling professionals to recognize and understand their emotions and reactions to various situations. This heightened self-awareness facilitates better interpersonal relationships, conflict resolution, and empathy towards colleagues and clients. Taking time for self-reflection allows the mind to wander, making room for creative ideas and innovative solutions to emerge. Professionals can tap into their creative potential by engaging in activities that promote reflection, such as journaling or engaging in open-ended discussions.

When it comes to Balancing Work and Personal Life Self-reflection encourages professionals to assess their work-life balance, ensuring that their personal well-being is not sacrificed for career achievements. By examining the allocation of time and energy, individuals can adjust strike a healthier equilibrium. Setting and Revising Goals Self-reflection provides an opportunity to set and review professional goals. Regularly reassessing objectives allows professionals to adapt to changing circumstances, stay focused on their priorities, and remain aligned with their long-term vision.

Cultivating Leadership Skills Effective leaders prioritize self-reflection, recognizing its role in developing authentic leadership styles. By understanding their leadership strengths and areas for growth, individuals can lead with empathy, inspire their teams, and create a positive work culture. Celebrating Accomplishments Self-reflection encourages professionals to acknowledge their accomplishments and celebrate their successes, no matter how small. Celebrating achievements boosts morale and motivates further progress.

Remember, finding inspiration is a personal journey, and different methods may resonate with different individuals. Experiment with various strategies to see what works best for you in rekindling your motivation and overcoming burnout. Prioritizing self-care and well-being are essential during this process to ensure sustainable and fulfilling success in your personal and professional life.

"Knowing yourself is the beginning of all wisdom." *-Aristotle*

**Things to Consider:**

1. **Take a Break:** Step away from your usual routine and allow yourself some time to rest and recharge. Engage in activities that you enjoy, whether it's spending time in nature, reading a book, or pursuing a hobby.

2. **Seek Support:** Talk to friends, family, or colleagues who understand and empathize with your situation. Sharing your feelings can provide emotional support and a fresh perspective.

3. **Reflect on Past Successes:** Remind yourself of the achievements and triumphs you've experienced in the past. Reflecting on your successes can boost your confidence and motivation.

4. **Practice Mindfulness:** Engage in mindfulness practices like meditation or deep breathing exercises to reduce stress and bring awareness to the present moment.

5. **Seek Inspirational Content:** Watch motivational videos, read books or articles that inspire you, or listen to podcasts that share stories of resilience and success.

6. **Connect with Inspirational Figures:** Seek out inspiring individuals in your field or other areas of interest. Learn from their experiences and absorb their passion and dedication.

7. **Attend Workshops or Seminars:** Participate in workshops or seminars related to your profession or interests. Engaging with like-minded individuals and learning from experts can reignite your passion.

8. **Explore New Avenues:** Consider exploring new interests or activities outside of your regular work. Trying something different can stimulate creativity and inspire new ideas.

9. **Set Short-term Goals:** Instead of focusing on long-term objectives, set smaller, achievable goals that can provide a sense of accomplishment and progress.

10. **Surround Yourself with Positivity**: Spend time with positive and supportive individuals who uplift your spirits and encourage you to overcome challenges.

11. **Keep a Journal:** Write down your thoughts and feelings regularly to process your emotions and gain clarity about your situation. This can help you identify patterns and triggers for

burnout.

12. **Practice Self-Compassion:** Be kind to yourself and acknowledge that burnout is a common experience. Treat yourself with the same compassion you would extend to a friend facing similar challenges.

13. **Seek Professional Help:** If burnout is severe or persistent, consider seeking help from a mental health professional who can provide guidance and support.

# CHAPTER 8

# COMMUNITY CONNECTION

"You may not control all the events that happen to you, but you can decide not to be reduced by them."
*-Maya Angelou*

Imagine yourself in an isolated room, burdened with all the challenges and stress that your profession entails. As days go by, the weight becomes unbearable, and eventually, burnout consumes you. We have all been there, experiencing the toll that work can take on our mental and emotional well-being. However, there is a solution that lies within our reach: connecting with others in our professional community. In this chapter, we will explore the significance of building relationships within our industry, creating a support network that acts as a shield against burnout.

The importance of staying connected with others in your professional community is significant when in steady journey against BURNOUT. It provides emotional support, facilitates learning, enables collaborative problem-solving, fosters accountability and motivation, and offers mentorship opportunities. Building relationships and forming networks within your professional community can significantly contribute to managing and preventing burnout.

Building relationships with colleagues who understand your professional challenges can provide emotional support. Sharing experiences, venting frustrations, and seeking advice and guidance can help alleviate the feelings of burnout. Knowing that you're not alone in your struggles can provide a significant boost to your morale. Networking with professionals in your community exposes you to different perspectives, ideas, and experiences. Engaging with others who have faced similar challenges can provide valuable insights and alternative approaches to managing work-related stress. It allows you to learn from their mistakes and successes, enhancing your ability to tackle burnout effectively.

Collaborating and connecting with others in your professional community creates opportunities for collaborative problem-solving. Working together, sharing ideas, and seeking input from your peers can help you find creative solutions to the causes of burnout. Collaboration fosters a sense of unity and collective effort, which can reduce the burden on individuals and contribute to a healthier work environment. Connecting with like-minded professionals fosters a sense of accountability. Engaging in discussions about professional growth, setting goals, and tracking progress together can keep you motivated and focused. Being a part of a supportive community can help you stay on track and prevent burnout by encouraging you to prioritize self-care and maintain a healthy work-life balance.

Engaging with others in your professional community can provide access to valuable mentorship opportunities or allow you to be a mentor yourself. Mentoring relationships contributes positively to personal and professional development, offering guidance, knowledge-sharing, and support. Having a mentor can help you navigate the complexities of your career and provide guidance in managing burnout effectively.

In a fast-paced professional world characterized by growing demands, burnout has become an all-too-common enemy. However, by embracing the power of connection, we can triumph over burnout. Connecting with others in our professional community fosters empathy, understanding, and a sense of belonging, while building a strong support network that benefits both our personal and professional lives. As we share experiences, collaborate, and nurture well-being, we can ensure that burnout becomes a hurdle easily attainable and not an ever-present threat. Remember, you are not alone—reach out, connect, and together let us create a community of resilience, progress, and fulfillment.

"Live as if you were to die tomorrow. Learn as if you were to live forever." – **Mahatma Gandhi**

**Things to consider as you network/connect with other professionals:**

1. **Common Interests and Goals:** Seek connections with individuals who share common interests, goals, or career aspirations. Having shared passions can facilitate more engaging and purposeful conversations.

2. **Mutual Benefit:** Look for opportunities to create mutually beneficial relationships. Networking should be a two-way street, where both parties can contribute and gain value from the connection.

3. **Authenticity:** Be genuine and authentic in your interactions. People appreciate sincerity and are more likely to connect with you when they feel you are being true to yourself.

4. **Active Listening:** Practice active listening when engaging with others. Pay attention to what they say, show interest in their experiences and perspectives, and respond thoughtfully.

5. **Positive Attitude:** Maintain a positive and enthusiastic attitude when connecting with your professional community. Positivity is infectious and can help create a welcoming and enjoyable networking environment.

6. **Professionalism:** Display professionalism in your interactions,

whether in person, online, or through email. Treat others with respect and always maintain a courteous demeanor.

7. **Diverse Perspectives:** Seek connections with individuals from diverse backgrounds and fields. Exposure to varied perspectives can broaden your horizons and enrich your professional experience.

8. **Contribution to the Community:** Look for ways to contribute to the professional community you are a part of. Participate in discussions, share valuable insights, and help when possible.

9. **Networking Events and Conferences:** Attend networking events, conferences, and industry-related gatherings to meet new people and expand your network. Such events provide excellent opportunities for meaningful connections.

10. **Utilize Online Platforms:** Engage with professional communities on social media platforms like LinkedIn, where you can connect with like-minded individuals, join groups, and participate in discussions.

11. **Follow Up:** After initial interactions, follow up with those you connect with to maintain the relationship. Reach out with a personalized message or email to stay in touch and continue building the connection.

12. **Supportive Relationships:** Seek to establish supportive relationships where you can lean on and provide support to others in your professional community. Building a network of supportive colleagues can be invaluable in times of need.

13. **Collaborative Opportunities:** Look for potential collaboration opportunities with individuals in your network. Collaboration can lead to new projects, ventures, or shared learning experiences.

14. **Stay Updated:** Keep yourself informed about the latest trends, news, and developments in your industry or field. Staying

updated allows you to contribute to discussions and stay relevant in your professional community.

15. **Time Management:** While networking is essential, manage your time wisely. Focus on building quality connections rather than trying to connect with everyone. Invest time in nurturing meaningful relationships.

# CHAPTER 9

# VACATION

"I have never believed that vacations are luxuries. They are our
necessities–just like shelter, clothes, and food. They make us feel like
humans and not like animals that care only for survival." —
*Alexander Babinets*

In today's highly demanding world of, burnout has become a prevalent
and concerning issue affecting individuals across various professions.
The relentless pressure to perform, meet deadlines, and maintain a high
level of productivity can lead to physical and emotional exhaustion. In
this essay, we delve into the crucial importance of taking vacations to
combat burnout effectively. By understanding the impact of vacations on
our well-being, work performance, and overall quality of life, we can
recognize the value of regular vacations in preventing burnout.

Taking vacations provides a much-needed opportunity for physical
and mental rejuvenation. Stepping away from the daily grind allows our
bodies to recover from stress and exhaustion. Vacations grant the mind
a respite from constant work-related thoughts, promoting mental clarity
and improved focus. These restorative effects help replenish energy

levels and prevent the physical and emotional toll that leads to burnout.

Vacations play a critical role in reducing stress levels. Removing ourselves from the workplace environment allows us to disconnect from the sources of stress and tension, providing a chance to unwind and relax. During vacations, our bodies release stress-reducing hormones, helping to restore a sense of balance and emotional well-being. By experiencing lower stress levels, we can build resilience and better cope with the demands of our professional lives. The concept of work-life balance has gained increasing recognition as an essential aspect of overall well-being. Taking vacations helps us strike a healthier equilibrium between our personal and professional commitments. By dedicating time to our personal lives, nurturing relationships, and engaging in leisure activities, we foster a sense of fulfillment beyond work-related achievements. A balanced life is instrumental in warding off burnout and preserving a sense of contentment.

Vacations provide a conducive environment for enhancing creativity and problem-solving skills. Stepping away from routine and exposing ourselves to new experiences and surroundings can inspire fresh perspectives and innovative ideas. The mental space and freedom from day-to-day pressures allow our minds to engage in creative thinking, leading to improved problem-solving abilities when we return to work. Taking vacations directly correlates with improved job performance. Regular breaks enable us to recharge and return to work with a renewed sense of enthusiasm and motivation. Well-rested individuals exhibit heightened productivity, a greater capacity to handle challenges, and an increased ability to maintain focus and concentration. A positive work environment is fostered, ultimately enhancing overall job satisfaction.

Vacationing is paramount to avoid burnout, maintain mental and emotional well-being, and sustain healthy personal relationships. By understanding the consequences of neglecting time off, embracing the benefits of vacations, and implementing effective strategies, individuals can find the necessary balance between work and leisure. Prioritizing and planning for vacations will not only lead to increased job satisfaction but also enhance overall quality of life. So, embark on your next adventure, recharge, and return to your professional endeavors with renewed energy and enthusiasm.

Taking vacations is not an indulgence or a luxury, but a fundamental need for maintaining a healthy and sustainable professional life. The importance of regular breaks for avoiding burnout cannot be overstated. By investing in vacations, we invest in our physical and mental well-being, nurture work-life balance, and fortify our professional performance. Vacations offer us the opportunity to step back, recharge, and return to our endeavors with renewed vigor and creativity. Recognizing the significance of taking vacations empowers us to protect ourselves from burnout, ensuring a fulfilling and successful journey both personally and professionally.

"Vacation is an opportunity to embrace your true self, whether that means finding rest and relaxation, pursuing personal growth, or simply enjoying life's pleasures."

**— Shabira Banu Hussain Sumbhaniya**

**Things to Consider when planning a Vacation to avoid Burnout:**

1. **Destination Selection:** Choose a destination that offers relaxation and serenity. Choose a place known for its tranquil environment, natural beauty, or activities that align with your interests and provide a sense of calm.

2. **Duration:** Plan an adequate duration for your vacation. Ensure it is long enough to allow for a complete break from work-related stress and responsibilities.

3. **Disconnect from Work**: Commit to disconnecting from work-related communication and conversations during your vacation. Set clear boundaries with colleagues and clients to avoid interruptions.

4. **Prioritize Rest:** Design your itinerary to include plenty of

downtime for relaxation and rest. Avoid overpacking your schedule with activities, leaving room for spontaneous moments of leisure.

5. **Engage in Mindful Activities:** Consider incorporating mindfulness practices into your vacation, such as yoga, meditation, or nature walks. These activities can help alleviate stress and promote mental clarity.

6. **Avoid Overstimulation:** If you are feeling overwhelmed, avoid destinations or activities that may exacerbate your stress. Choose serene locations and gentle experiences to promote calmness.

7. **Seek Opportunities for Solitude:** Find opportunities for solitude during your trip. Moments of quiet reflection can help you reconnect with yourself and recharge your emotional batteries.

8. **Set Realistic Expectations:** Recognize that a vacation may not solve all your burnout-related challenges. Set realistic expectations and allow yourself to embrace the process of recovery.

9. **Travel with Supportive Companions:** If you're traveling with others, choose supportive companions who understand your need for rest and are respectful of your boundaries.

10. **Pack Light:** Minimize the burden of travel by packing only the essentials. Traveling light will reduce stress and make the journey more manageable.

11. **Limit Screen Time:** Reduce screen time and avoid engaging in work-related activities on your electronic devices. Instead, focus on being present in the moment and enjoying your surroundings.

12. **Engage in Activities That Bring Joy:** Prioritize activities that bring you joy and pleasure, whether it's reading a book, exploring nature, or trying new cuisines.

13. **Avoid Over-Planning:** Allow room for spontaneity and

flexibility in your trip. Avoid rigid itineraries that may add unnecessary pressure during your vacation.

14. **Embrace Slow Travel:** Consider adopting a slow travel approach, which allows you to immerse yourself in the destination and experience it at a relaxed pace.

15. **Practice Gratitude:** Take time each day to express gratitude for the opportunity to take a vacation and for the positive experiences you encounter during your trip.

# CHAPTER 10

# DIET AND EXERCISE

"Physical fitness is not only one of the most important keys to a healthy body, but also the basis of dynamic and creative intellectual activity." - *John F. Kennedy*

In the modern world, burnout has become a progressive issue, affecting individuals across various professions and walks of life. The relentless demands of work, combined with the pressures of daily living, can take a toll on our physical and mental well-being. In this chapter, we explore the powerful impact of clean eating, a balanced diet, and regular exercise on preventing burnout. By nourishing our bodies with wholesome foods and engaging in physical activity, we can fortify our resilience, boost energy levels, and foster a healthier mindset to combat burnout effectively.

Clean eating, which focuses on consuming whole, unprocessed foods, provides essential nutrients for the mind and body. By fueling ourselves with vitamins, minerals, and antioxidants, we support cognitive function, mental clarity, and overall vitality. Proper nutrition enhances our ability to handle stress and helps ward off the physical and emotional exhaustion that leads to burnout. A well-balanced diet and clean eating habits lead to increased energy levels. Consuming nutritious foods provides a steady and sustained source of energy, preventing energy crashes and fatigue. As a result, individuals experience heightened productivity and greater capacity to meet the demands of their professional and personal lives.

Proper nutrition plays a crucial role in mood regulation. Balanced meals that include healthy fats, lean proteins, and complex carbohydrates contribute to stable blood sugar levels, reducing mood swings and irritability. A positive mood can foster a more resilient mindset, helping individuals cope with stress and challenges more effectively. Physical activity, such as regular exercise, is a potent stress-reducer. Engaging in activities like walking, running, yoga, or dancing triggers the release of endorphins, which are natural mood boosters. Exercise also helps alleviate tension and anxiety, offering a much-needed break from work-related stress.

A combination of clean eating and regular exercise positively impacts sleep quality. Proper nutrition and physical activity contribute to a more restful and rejuvenating sleep, allowing the body and mind to recover fully from daily stressors. Quality sleep is essential for preventing burnout and maintaining overall well-being. Clean eating and regular exercise build resilience, both physically and mentally. Strengthening the body through nutritious foods and physical activity enables individuals to better cope with stressors and bounce back from challenging situations.

Proper nutrition and regular exercise support a robust immune system. A strong immune system helps ward off illnesses and infections, reducing the risk of falling sick during times of heightened stress, which can further contribute to burnout. Clean eating and exercise foster a positive body-mind connection. As individuals take care of their bodies, they become more attuned to their overall well-being, which can lead to greater self-awareness and mindfulness in managing stress and avoiding burnout.

Combining poor diet and no exercise creates a vicious cycle that exacerbates burnout. A lack of nutritious food weakens the body's ability to cope with stress, lowers resistance to illnesses, and reduces energy levels, making it harder to engage in physical activity. Simultaneously, a sedentary lifestyle decreases motivation to eat healthy, promotes quick and unhealthy eating habits, and further magnifies the negative impact on overall well-being. As a result, both poor dietary choices and lack of exercise contribute to a downward spiral that worsens burnout symptoms and decreases an individual's ability to recover from it.

Clean eating, a balanced diet, and regular exercise are powerful allies in the fight against burnout. Nourishing our bodies with wholesome foods and engaging in physical activity promotes mental clarity, enhanced energy, and resilience in the face of stress. These practices not only prevent burnout but also foster a holistic approach to well-being, enabling individuals to thrive both personally and professionally. Embracing clean eating, a balanced diet, and regular exercise empowers us to create a sustainable and fulfilling lifestyle that supports our physical, emotional, and mental health, laying the foundation for long-term success and happiness.

"If you really want to make a friend, go to someone's house and eat... The people who give you their food give you, their heart." – *Cesar Chavez*

**Things to consider:**

1. **Walking:** Take regular walks outdoors to get fresh air and clear your mind. Walking is a low-impact exercise that can be easily incorporated into your daily routine.

2. **Yoga:** Practice yoga to improve flexibility, reduce tension, and promote relaxation. Yoga combines physical movements with mindfulness, making it an excellent stress-relieving activity.

3. **Meditation:** Engage in meditation to calm your mind, reduce anxiety, and enhance focus. Meditation can be done in various forms, such as mindfulness meditation or guided visualization.

4. **Cardiovascular Exercises:** Incorporate cardiovascular exercises like jogging, cycling, or swimming to increase heart rate and boost endorphins, which are natural mood lifters.

5. **Strength Training:** Incorporate strength training exercises like weightlifting or bodyweight exercises to build muscle strength and improve overall body composition.

6. **Pilates:** Try Pilates to improve core strength, flexibility, and posture. Pilates is a gentle exercise that can be beneficial for relieving tension in the body.

7. **Dancing:** Dancing is a fun way to stay active while improving coordination and reducing stress. Put on some music and let yourself move freely.

8. **Stretching:** Practice stretching exercises regularly to reduce muscle tension and improve flexibility.

9. **Balanced Meals:** Aim for balanced meals that include a combination of lean proteins, whole grains, healthy fats, and a variety of fruits and vegetables.

10. **Hydration:** Stay well-hydrated by drinking plenty of water throughout the day. Dehydration can exacerbate feelings of fatigue and stress.

11. **Mindful Eating:** Practice mindful eating by savoring each bite and paying attention to hunger and fullness cues. Avoid eating while distracted or under stress.

12. **Regular Mealtimes:** Establish regular mealtimes to promote a consistent and healthy eating routine.

13. **Reduce Processed Foods:** Minimize the consumption of processed and high-sugar foods, which can lead to energy crashes and worsen stress levels.

14. **Healthy Snacks:** Keep nutritious snacks on hand, such as nuts, fruits, yogurt, or vegetable sticks, to avoid reaching for unhealthy

options when feeling stressed.

15. **Limit Caffeine and Alcohol:** While moderate consumption of caffeine and alcohol is acceptable, excessive intake can disrupt sleep and exacerbate stress.

16. **Cook at Home:** Cooking at home allows you to control ingredients and portion sizes, making it easier to maintain a balanced diet.

# CHAPTER 11

# LEARN TO SAY "NO"

"The difference between successful people and really successful people is that really successful people say no to almost everything." - *Warren Buffett*

In the fast-paced and demanding world of entrepreneurship, artistry, and business, the pressure to say "yes" to every opportunity can be overwhelming. However, this constant pursuit of more can lead to burnout, affecting creativity, productivity, and overall well-being. Learning to say "no" strategically and assertively is a vital skill to maintain a healthy work-life balance and prevent the dreaded burnout. In this chapter, we will explore the importance of setting boundaries, understanding priorities, and embracing the power of saying "no."

Before we delve into learning to say "no," it is essential to recognize the warning signs of burnout. As driven professionals, we often push ourselves to the limit, not realizing that we are heading toward exhaustion. Signs of burnout include chronic fatigue, decreased productivity, feelings of cynicism, detachment, and even physical symptoms like headaches and insomnia. By being aware of these signs, entrepreneurs, artists, and business professionals can take early action to protect themselves from burnout.

The first step in mastering the art of saying "no" is to establish clear goals and priorities. Whether you're an entrepreneur working on a new venture, an artist pursuing creative projects, or a business professional managing multiple responsibilities, knowing your long-term objectives allows you to filter opportunities that align with your vision. Setting priorities will enable you to focus on projects that truly matter and decline distractions that can lead to burnout.

Not every opportunity that comes your way is worth pursuing. Learning to identify red flags in potential ventures or collaborations can save you from unnecessary stress and exhaustion. Common red flags include unrealistic expectations, excessive time commitments, misalignment with your values, or projects that don't contribute to your long-term goals. Embrace the power of critical evaluation to recognize opportunities that may lead you down the path of burnout.

Saying "no" is not about being rude or uncooperative; it's about setting boundaries and preserving your well-being. Politeness and clarity are key when declining opportunities. Politely expressing gratitude for the offer and explaining your decision firmly yet respectfully will help maintain professional relationships. Additionally, providing a reason for your decision can help others understand your perspective and respect your choice.

Fear of Missing Out (FOMO) can be a significant driver behind the reluctance to say "no." However, it's essential to recognize that every opportunity comes with an opportunity cost. Embrace the idea that saying "no" to certain ventures allows you to say "yes" to more meaningful and fulfilling experiences. Letting go of FOMO enables you to focus on what truly matters and avoid spreading yourself too thin.

As an entrepreneur, artist, or business professional, you may feel the need to take on everything yourself. However, recognizing that you don't have to do it all is crucial for preventing burnout. Delegating tasks to capable team members or collaborating with others not only lightens your workload but also promotes a sense of collective accomplishment. Trusting others with responsibilities fosters a healthier work environment and allows you to focus on tasks that require your expertise.

Prioritizing self-care is a non-negotiable aspect of avoiding burnout. As you learn to say "no" to overcommitment, ensure that you say "yes" to taking care of yourself. Regular exercise, sufficient sleep, and moments of relaxation are essential for recharging your mind and body. Engaging in activities that bring joy and fulfillment outside of work contributes to a more balanced and sustainable lifestyle.

Learning when to say "no" is an invaluable skill for entrepreneurs, artists, and business professionals seeking to avoid burnout. Recognizing the signs of burnout, setting clear goals, and identifying red flags in potential opportunities are essential steps to protect your well-being. Embracing the power of saying "no" politely and firmly empowers you to focus on projects aligned with your vision and values.

By overcoming the fear of missing out, delegating tasks, and prioritizing self-care, you can maintain a healthy work-life balance, unleash creativity, and thrive in your chosen profession. Remember, saying "no" today may open doors to even greater opportunities tomorrow, allowing you to achieve sustainable success in your entrepreneurial, artistic, or business journey!

"No is a complete sentence. It does not require an explanation to follow. You can truly answer someone's request with a simple no." - *Sharon E. Rainey*

**Professional ways to say "No" to distractions:**

1. "Thank you for considering me, but I'm currently fully committed to other projects. I won't be able to take on any additional tasks at the moment."

2. "I appreciate the opportunity, but I need to prioritize my existing responsibilities and can't commit to this new endeavor."

3. "I've reviewed the request, and while it sounds exciting, I must decline as it doesn't align with my current business objectives."

4. "I'm honored that you thought of me for this collaboration. Unfortunately, my schedule is booked, and I won't be able to participate."

5. "I understand the importance of this task, but my plate is already quite full, and I wouldn't want to compromise the quality of my existing work."

6. "I'm flattered by the invitation, but I have to respectfully decline as I'm focusing on a critical project right now."

7. "I value our working relationship, but I'm unable to take on any additional commitments at this time."

8. "I need to prioritize self-care and balance in my life, so I won't be able to engage in this opportunity."

9. "I appreciate your understanding that my current workload prevents me from taking on extra responsibilities."

10. "Given my current commitments, I must decline, but I hope we can collaborate in the future when my schedule allows."

11. "I'm dedicated to achieving our team's goals, and I believe saying 'no' to this distraction is the best way to maintain our focus."

12. "While I understand the urgency of this matter, I must stay focused on my current projects to ensure their successful completion."

13. "Thank you for thinking of me, but I have to decline to ensure I can continue delivering high-quality work on my existing tasks."

14. "I've carefully evaluated the distraction's potential benefits, but it doesn't align with my long-term vision for my business/career."

15. "I'm grateful for the opportunity, but my current professional commitments require my undivided attention."

# CHAPTER 12

# WHEN TO SAY "YES" TO HELP

The person who is willing to say yes to experience is the person who discovers new frontiers.
*-John Templeton*

As entrepreneurs, artists, and business professionals, the desire to achieve success often drives us to take on numerous responsibilities and wear multiple hats. While determination and self-reliance are essential traits, the misconception that we must handle everything on our own can lead to burnout. Learning when to say "yes" to help can be a game-changer in maintaining a healthy work-life balance and preventing burnout. In this chapter, we will explore the benefits of accepting help, ways to delegate effectively, and the power of building a supportive network.

In the competitive world of entrepreneurship, artistry, and business, the notion of the lone wolf – an individual who tackles every challenge alone – is often romanticized. However, this mindset can be detrimental to one's well-being. Embracing help and collaboration doesn't make you weak; it demonstrates strength in acknowledging your limitations and recognizing that teamwork can lead to greater success.

Before delving into the art of accepting help, it's crucial to recognize the signs of overwhelm. Persistent stress, declining productivity, and a feeling of being spread too thin are red flags indicating that you may need assistance. Acknowledging these signs is the first step toward creating a healthier approach to your work.

Delegation is the superhero power that can free up your time, reduce stress, and boost productivity. Learning to delegate effectively involves identifying tasks that others can handle without compromising quality. Trusting your team members or hiring specialists allows you to focus on your strengths while ensuring that each aspect of your business or artistic venture receives the attention it deserves.

Asking for help doesn't mean seeking assistance from just anyone. Identifying the right individuals to support your vision is crucial. Surround yourself with trustworthy and reliable team members, mentors, or advisors who share your passion and align with your goals. Building a supportive network can provide invaluable guidance and encouragement during challenging times.

A common barrier to accepting help is the fear of losing control over your projects. As an entrepreneur, artist, or business professional, it's essential to recognize that delegating tasks doesn't equate to losing ownership. Communicate clearly with your team, set expectations, and provide guidance while allowing them the autonomy to excel. Embracing collaboration can lead to creative breakthroughs and innovative solutions.

Mentorship is a transformative relationship that can significantly impact personal and professional growth. Accepting help from mentors allows you to learn from their experiences, gain new perspectives, and avoid common pitfalls. Whether it's seeking guidance from seasoned entrepreneurs, successful artists, or experienced business professionals, mentorship can provide invaluable insights that accelerate your journey.

As you embrace the power of accepting help, striking a balance between independence and interdependence becomes crucial. Cultivating a sense of self-reliance is essential, but it should be complemented by a willingness to collaborate and accept support when needed. The ability to balance these aspects fosters resilience and adaptability. Saying "yes" to help also involves prioritizing self-care. Recognize that taking care of your physical and mental well-being enables you to be at your best, both personally and professionally. Make time for activities that recharge your energy, whether it's exercise, spending time with loved ones, or engaging in hobbies. A well-nourished mind and body are better equipped to handle challenges and prevent burnout.

In the journey of entrepreneurship, artistry, and business, saying "yes" to help is not a sign of weakness but a reflection of wisdom. Recognizing when to delegate, accepting guidance, and building a supportive network empowers you to avoid burnout and achieve sustainable success. Embrace the power of collaboration, foster a culture of support, and prioritize self-care to flourish as an entrepreneur, artist, or business professional. Remember, the journey to success is not meant to be traveled alone; the strength of a community can propels you to greater heights.

What is no? Either you have asked the wrong question, or you have asked the wrong person. Find a way to get the 'yes'. – *Jeanette Winterson*

**Things to consider when Saying "Yes" to help:**

1. **Heavy Workload:** When you have an excessive workload that exceeds your capacity, accepting help allows you to distribute tasks and avoid burnout.

2. **Time Management:** Saying "yes" to help can improve time management by delegating non-core tasks, freeing up time for essential responsibilities.

3. **Focus on Core Competencies:** Accepting help allows you to focus on your core competencies and strategic decision-making,

leading to a more significant impact in your work.

4. **Personal Well-being:** Seeking assistance enables you to take care of your physical and mental health, reducing stress and the risk of burnout.

5. **Creative Block:** Collaborating with others can help overcome creative blocks, bringing fresh perspectives and inspiring new ideas.

6. **Project Deadlines:** When facing tight deadlines, accepting help ensures that projects are completed on time, reducing stress and pressure.

7. **Skill Augmentation:** Saying "yes" to help from individuals with complementary skills can enhance the quality of your work and lead to more robust outcomes.

8. **Opportunity to Learn:** Accepting help provides an opportunity to learn from others' expertise and experiences, fostering personal and professional growth.

9. **Networking and Collaboration:** Collaborating with others opens doors to new connections and potential partnerships, expanding your network and opportunities.

10. **Managing Multiple Ventures:** As an entrepreneur with multiple ventures, accepting help allows you to navigate diverse projects effectively.

11. **Support System:** Building a supportive team or network can provide encouragement during challenging times and reduce the burden on individuals.

12. **Business Expansion:** Saying "yes" to help can facilitate business expansion, whether through hiring additional staff or seeking external support.

13. **Customer Service:** Accepting help in customer service or support functions ensures that your customers receive prompt

and satisfactory assistance.

14. **Avoiding Micromanagement:** Trusting others to handle certain tasks allows you to avoid micromanaging and fosters a positive work environment.

15. **Resilience:** Seeking help demonstrates resilience and adaptability, recognizing that collaboration is key to long-term success.

16. **Preventing Overcommitment:** Accepting help helps you avoid overcommitment and spread yourself too thin, leading to better focus and effectiveness.

17. **Leveraging Specialized Knowledge:** Partnering with experts in specific areas can provide valuable insights and drive innovation.

18. **Reaching Goals Faster:** Saying "yes" to help accelerate progress toward your goals by tapping into additional resources and skills.

19. **Personal Growth**: Collaborating with others allows you to learn from diverse perspectives, contributing to personal and professional development.

20. **Team Building:** Accepting help and acknowledging contributions build a positive team culture, fostering mutual support and camaraderie.

# Conclusion

In the riveting conclusion of "Avoiding Burnout: A Guide for Entrepreneurs, Artists, and Business Professionals to Gain and Maintain Success," we stand at the precipice of a transformative journey—a journey that has taken us through the depths of burnout, the power of self-care, the art of setting realistic goals, and the harmony of work-life integration. As we reflect on the insights garnered from the experiences of resilient individuals and expert wisdom, one resounding truth emerges: success is not just about achieving milestones; it is about preserving our well-being and embracing a sustainable path to greatness.

In the finale, we celebrate the triumph of resilience—the unwavering spirit that propels us forward despite challenges and setbacks. We have learned that by acknowledging the importance of self-care and setting realistic goals, we fortify ourselves against burnout and cultivate a thriving foundation for success.

As entrepreneurs, artists, and business professionals, we have discovered that our personal well-being is not a luxury—it is the cornerstone of our journey to lasting success. Armed with the knowledge, wisdom, and tools within these pages, we are equipped to navigate the complexities of our professional lives while nurturing our physical, emotional, and mental health.

Let this book be a guiding light—a constant reminder to embrace self-compassion, cultivate resilience, and integrate our passions and personal lives harmoniously. As we step into the future, may "Avoiding

Burnout" be our steadfast ally, empowering us to achieve greatness without sacrificing our most valuable asset which is ourselves.

This is not just a conclusion; it is an invitation to embark on a lifelong commitment to well-being, success, and fulfillment. Together, let us conquer burnout and embrace a thriving and purposeful existence as we continue to make a lasting impact on the world.

The journey to success begins with self-care, and it is an extraordinary journey indeed.

Randy C. Reeves, II

# AUTHOR BIOGRAPHY

Randy C. Reeves, II, attended Southeastern Institute of Technology earning him a certification in Massage Therapy. He is also a member of (AMTA) The American Massage Therapy Association. As an accomplished full-time licensed massage therapist and part-time professional poker player, he brings a unique blend of holistic well-being and strategic skills to the pages of "Avoiding Burnout: A Guide for Entrepreneurs, Artists, and Business Professionals to Gain and Maintain Success." With an unwavering commitment to promoting wellness and a knack for strategic decision-making, Randy C. Reeves, II gives a fresh perspective on achieving lasting success while safeguarding one's physical, emotional, and mental vitality.

As a full-time licensed massage therapist, Randy C. Reeves, II has dedicated years to helping individuals find balance, relaxation, and renewal. With a compassionate touch and a deep understanding of the body's intricate connections, Mr. Reeves has nurtured the well-being of countless clients, instilling a profound appreciation for self-care and the importance of maintaining equilibrium in the face of life's challenges.

In the world of professional poker, Randy has honed the art of calculated risks and strategic thinking. With a keen ability to anticipate outcomes, navigate uncertainty, read situations, and body language Randy has not only achieved success at the poker table but also harnessed these skills to guide others toward making informed decisions in their personal and professional lives.

Through his debut novel "AVOIDING BURNUT" Randy C. Reeves, II bridges the gap between wellness and strategy, offering a comprehensive guide to preventing burnout and achieving harmonious success. By drawing from Randy's expertise as a licensed massage therapist and professional poker player, readers gain invaluable insights into effective goal setting, work-life integration, and the transformative power of self-care.

Embark on a transformative journey with Randy C. Reeves, II as a trusted guide, and unlock the secrets to sustaining success, cultivating resilience, and embracing a life of fulfillment.